Alfred's
Teach Yourself
Sonar

MW00571045

DAN WOTHKE

Everything you need to know to start recording now!

- **For beginners with no prior training**

- **Covers the basics of MIDI setup, loops, microphones, recording guitars & vocals, effects, mixing, and more**

- **DVD includes over 80 minutes of video lessons**

Alfred Music Publishing Co., Inc.
P.O. Box 10003
Van Nuys, CA 91410-0003
alfred.com

Copyright © MMX by Alfred Music Publishing Co., Inc.
All rights reserved. Printed in USA.

Produced in association with Lawson Music Media, Inc.

ISBN-10: 0-7390-6641-2 Book & DVD
ISBN-13: 978-0-7390-6641-6 Book & DVD

Cover photos: Electric guitar courtesy of Fender Musical Instruments • Electronic keyboard courtesy of Korg USA, Inc.

Edited by Mary Cosola.

 Alfred Cares. Contents printed on 100% recycled paper.

CONTENTS

INTRODUCTION

Cakewalk Sonar is a very powerful workstation and a fantastic program for recording and editing your songs. It takes what was once a very complicated process and makes it so simple that even the absolute beginner can dive right in and begin making professional-sounding recordings. Sonar has a wealth of audio features, sounds, effects and tools that allow you to turn your song ideas into excellent recordings, whether you plan to use your finished song as your latest download offering on a Website or burn it to a CD, create a video soundtrack, or anything else you can think of.

This book is designed for people who are new to recording, and to using Sonar in particular. In addition to explaining the ins and outs of Sonar, it will cover basic concepts about your PC, recording, audio/MIDI devices, microphones and more. But no matter how much music-recording experience you've had before you start using Sonar, you'll be on your way to making excellent-sounding recordings once you learn your way around.

We'll break down some fairly complex ideas into simple concepts that will leave you ready to turn your song ideas into great recordings. In general, the concepts explained in this book apply to any version of Sonar. The accompanying DVD provides visual examples of each process. Studying the book and DVD together will give you a solid foundation of knowledge to build upon when using Sonar to construct your recordings.

GETTING TO KNOW YOUR PC

Before installing Sonar, look closely at the computer handling recording. PCs come in all shapes and sizes, ranging from a basic model to a high-performance machine designed to take on high-end multimedia software. In choosing a system, the biggest factor is going to be your cost-for-computer-to-"I still need to eat" ratio. It would be great if you had $3,000 to spend on a machine built solely for the purpose of recording and production, but realistically, most users are looking to add or upgrade the recording capabilities on a multi-purpose machine. Personally, I have used Sonar on a wide array of systems, with mixed results. Start with a look at the computer system specs compared with the system requirements listed by Sonar.

Looking Under the Hood of Windows

Sonar is designed for the Windows platform and its many operating system versions. The first step in determining how Sonar will work best for you is to examine your PC and take an inventory of the three vital components where Sonar will require the greatest load: the processor (CPU), random access memory (RAM) and the hard drive space and speed of the hard drive.

I'll demonstrate this process using Windows 7, and I will refer to steps for Windows XP. (Windows Vista is very similar to Windows 7, as far as determining the system specifications.)

In Windows, go to the Start Menu and right-click on My Computer, then choose Properties (Fig. 1). This menu will give you a quick overview of your PC, including information about your CPU, RAM, operating system and system type.

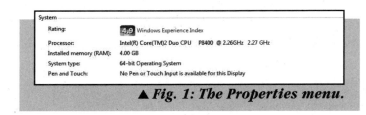

▲ *Fig. 1: The Properties menu.*

In the image here (Windows 7), the machine is running a Core 2 Duo with 4 GB of RAM and a 64-bit operating system. Compare this system to the requirements listed by Cakewalk for the latest version of Sonar, and it appears this system should handle running the software without any problems.

For a more detailed look at all of the system resources available to your computer, go to Start>All Programs>Accessories>System Tools>System Information (Windows XP); for a simplified method in Windows 7 and Vista, press Start and type in System Information (Fig. 2).

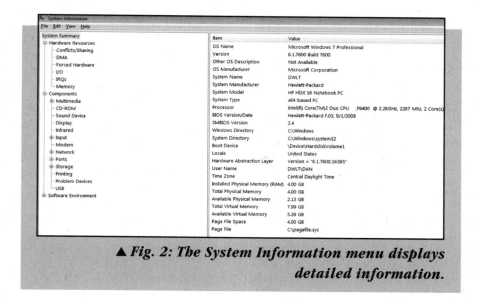

▲ *Fig. 2: The System Information menu displays detailed information.*

The Device Manager

The Device Manager is a one-stop overview of all hardware associated with your PC. This will show you which devices are behaving and which devices are having trouble loading the drivers. Here, you can also disable hardware so the system will ignore it. For example, on dedicated audio machines, I usually disable the onboard sound card to avoid any confusion when setting up my sound card options in Sonar. To access the Device Manager (Fig. 3), go to Start and type in Device Manager; in XP, you can find it in the Control Panel.

I highly recommend you spend some time getting familiar with your machine and learning your PC's properties. This will save you many headaches, such as buying a software package you can't run or can't run well, or trying to make a hardware device work with a machine that doesn't support it.

The amount of RAM you have and the speed of your processor directly relate to the performance of your software, the number of software instruments you can use and the number of audio tracks you can create while recording. In other words, don't expect to use an older PC with a 6-year old processor with the minimum amount of RAM and then set up 25–30 audio tracks and a bunch of virtual instruments; it just won't happen.

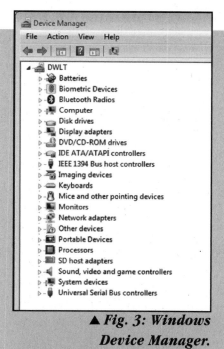

▲ *Fig. 3: Windows Device Manager.*

Granted, a lot of this information may look like gobbledygook right now—and don't worry, there won't be a follow-up quiz—but just remember that the Device Manager is a great place to get a quick glance at the processor, total RAM versus available RAM, system hardware (such as the DVD drive, which is required to install Sonar), hard drive speed and available disk space (located under Components >Storage>Drives; see Fig. 4).

As you can see, Cakewalk lists system recommendations and minimums to run Sonar. Obviously, the minimum requirements are just that: bare-bones requirements to use the software. Running Sonar on a system that barely covers the minimum would probably result in more frustration than creation, but if that is all you have, I will address maximizing your system's performance to squeeze every possible bit out and get the best results.

Operating System*
Windows XP SP3, Windows Vista SP2 (32 and 64-bit), or Windows 7 (32 and 64-bit)

Processor Speed
Minimum:
Intel Pentium 4 2.8 GHz [EMT64] or AMD Athlon XP 2800+ or higher

Recommended:
Intel Core 2 Quad Core Q8400 Yorkfield 2.66GHz or AMD Phenom Quad Core 9750 2.4GHz or higher

RAM
Minimum:
1 GB

Recommended:
4 GB

Graphics
Minimum:
1024 x 768, 16-bit color

Recommended:
1280 x 960, 24-bit color or higher

Hard Disk Space
Minimum:
200 MB (Minimal Installation) or higher

Recommended:
50 GB (Full Installation) or higher

Hard Disk Type
Minimum:
Any

Recommended:
EIDE / Ultra DMA (7200 RPM) or SATA

MIDI Interface**
Windows-compatible

Audio Interface***
Windows-compatible

Media Drive***
Dual Layer DVD-ROM, DVD+/- R, OR DVD+/-RW for installation/ CD-R OR CD-RW capability required for CD audio disc burning

Web Server Access***
Minimum:
Any

Recommended:
Available web server space with FTP access privileges

*SONAR does not officially support Windows 95, 98, ME, NT, 2000, XP x64 or pre-release (RTM) versions of Windows7

**Required to connect external MIDI devices

***Required for audio playback. See www.cakewalk.com/PCResource for a complete list of recommended audio devices.

****SONAR is presented on DVD media. DVD-ROM, DVD+/-R, or DVD+/-RW Drive required for installation

*****Cakewalk Publisher requires you to have available web server space with FTP access privileges. An internet connection is require for music uploading. A broadband connection is recommended.

▲ *Fig. 4: Sonar system recommendations.*

Take note of the supported operating systems. Here, nothing older than Windows XP with Service Pack 3 applied will run this version of Sonar (8.5 at time of print). Neither will any version of Windows XP 64-bit, which is rarely used. Vista requires SP2, and both Vista and 7 will work in 32-bit or 64-bit mode. As updates and patches are applied, supported operating systems will also evolve.

Windows, as with all software, is constantly releasing patches and updates. It is best to check your system compatibility before applying updates. This task can feel like chasing a moving target because if your system is running other applications in addition to Sonar, those titles may also require updates—not to mention dealing with security concerns and patching holes. The key is to frequently back up your system drive to an external drive. This way, if a system crashes or stops working, you can get your system back to a stable state from a previous point in time. Windows offers a System Restore feature, which works well, but it can tax background system resources.

CHAPTER 2 MIDI INTRODUCTION

Now that we've examined what it takes to run Sonar and talked a little bit about your PC's processing power and memory requirements, I will cover some of the ways that you can record sound with Sonar. Let's start by learning about MIDI.

MIDI, which stands for Musical Instrument Digital Interface, transmits musical information as data into a sequencing program, which in turn triggers sounds assigned to that data and plays them back according to how the data was originally input. In other words, MIDI records and transmits data instructions for notes, velocity, volume and other aspects of the performance. In the past, MIDI was much more complicated, and sequencers were difficult-to-use hardware devices that talked to sound sources such as synthesizers and samplers via the MIDI connection. These days MIDI is much easier to use, due partly to the development of USB connectivity and software-based synthesizers, samplers, and other virtual instruments controlled completely in your PC.

Simply put, digital audio is different than MIDI because a MIDI track has data in it that tells the track what to play from a sound source, whereas an audio track plays the actual audio recorded on the track. MIDI data can be manipulated in nearly infinite ways, whereas audio manipulations are much more limited. In other words, MIDI does not record sound itself, but data to tell the computer which notes should be played for whichever sound you assign to the track. This means you can play a part as a piano and go back later and decide to make the exact same performance now sound like an organ or any other instrument, just by changing the assigned sound rather than replaying the part with a new sound assigned.

With the exception of some new waveform-manipulation software just hitting the market, audio is typically a what-you-hear-is-what-you-get experience until you add effects like delay, reverb and compression to shape the actual recording into something different. MIDI data, on the other hand, can be changed in innumerable ways very easily, and even a beginner can make changes within Sonar.

Synths in Sonar

So where will your sounds come from in Sonar? The program differentiates between recording software instruments and "real" instruments, and routes MIDI tracks to synthesizer tracks to generate the actual sounds. (I'll get into track-level connection and setting of these devices later in the book; for now, let's make sure you have a basic understanding of the hardware you'll want to own to get sound into your PC and Sonar.)

A MIDI device generates data into Sonar using a piano-style keyboard (Fig. 5) or, if you're brave, a MIDI guitar or wind controller or other MIDI input device, or by manually drawing in the notes. For the purposes of this book and accompanying DVD, we're going to assume that you are using a simple MIDI keyboard connected to your PC. (If you choose to use a different type of MIDI controller, the same principles will apply.)

▲ *Fig. 5: Keyboard MIDI controller*

To get sound and MIDI data into Sonar, you'll need both a MIDI device and an audio device. Often you'll get a device that provides both MIDI and audio capabilities in one unit, both of which can support USB or Firewire, but MIDI devices never come as stand-alone Firewire devices. Your best bet is to choose an affordable, quality audio device that has both MIDI and audio connections.

You have a world of choices, from simple 2-channel audio devices to complex audio devices. You can purchase a simple keyboard with a small octave range and no internal sounds, which sends only MIDI data via USB, for less than $100, and this can more than suffice for getting ideas and parts into your songs. If you don't use a USB MIDI keyboard or an audio device with MIDI built into it, you will have to buy a simple one-input USB MIDI device that connects to your PC and connect the output of your MIDI controller into it.

I encourage you to visit a local musical instrument retailer that has a healthy pro audio recording department. By visiting a store that specializes in recording, you'll likely be able to choose from a better equipment selection and find more knowledgeable staff to advise you on which device suits your needs best. It is possible to get started without spending much money on an audio device or a MIDI device. For example, your PC may come with a built-in audio input that allows you to plug in a microphone or even a guitar, and record audio from a PC's built-in microphone or line input. However, these options aren't great ideas for anything beyond capturing a quick song idea into Sonar.

Arm yourself with an affordable, good-quality audio/MIDI capturing device and a MIDI input instrument that you're comfortable playing, and you'll be on your way to making great tracks in no time!

In the next chapter, we'll cover the variety of audio devices available for capturing instruments and allow you to connect a microphone to your PC.

AUDIO AND MIDI DEVICES

Sonar offers various options for getting audio into the system. The most basic options are plugging into your PC's own input or using the built-in microphone on your PC, but for audio-quality reasons, I don't recommend either of these. A better choice is to use an audio device, which will allow you to directly connect a microphone or an instrument and bring that analog source into your computer as digital information which can be stored, manipulated and played back.

Choosing the Right Audio Device— and a Word about USB

USB and Firewire are interface specifications for external devices—for our purposes, audio and MIDI devices—to connect with our computers. These are common interfaces for printers, scanners, external devices, etc. At the time of writing, USB v2 is by far the most common interface. Firewire, although it can boast similar and even better speeds (Fig. 6), is used less, as USB is an open format.

	USB		FireWire	
	1.1	2.0	400	800
Data transfer rate	12 Mbps	480 Mbps	400 Mbps	800 Mbps

▲ *Fig. 6: USB/Firewire speed comparison*

How many audio tracks do you want to record at the same time: One? Two? More? Think about that before you purchase your audio device. If you're a guitar player and you plan to record stereo guitar mics and a vocal at the same time, you'll need to be able to send three inputs simultaneously to Sonar. This is important to consider up front, because your choice of audio device and connection interface will determine how many simultaneous tracks you can record. If you want to record your voice only, guitar only or any other sound into one mono track at a time, then a simple stereo-interface audio device will get you started with Sonar just fine. If you want to record a set of drums and record each microphone input on a separate track, you'll have to step up from a USB v1.1 device to a USB v2 or Firewire device, which allow for more than two tracks to be recorded at once, each to a separate track.

Audio devices come in several connection choices, the most common being Firewire and USB. Typically, PCI cards are more commonly found in older PCs, with newer machines housing a PCIe slot on the motherboard. The great thing about these configurations is they provide you with a way to add connectivity to your computer. If you only have USB 1 a PCI/PCIe card can add USB 2 or Firewire ports to your system. This can add one more level of complexity to the compatibility issue, but most PCI cards that are compatible with your PC are invisible to the audio interface, meaning the audio interface is not aware that there is a separate device connected between it and the computer.

In any case, these cards connect to a box that either sits on your desktop or installs in a rack. Box styles vary from model to model and manufacturer to manufacturer; this is another reason why it's a great idea to consult a knowledgeable salesperson at a music instrument retailer while armed with your computer model's specs. Don't rely 100 percent on the salespeople, they are there to sell, and while they hopefully know what they're talking about, they are not always up on every issue. So before you make your purchase, do some research; put your potential audio/MIDI devices and your OS version into Google or another Web search engine along with the words "problems" and "trouble," and see what pops up.

I have experienced compatibility issues, and nothing puts the kibosh on a creative workflow than technical a problem caused by incompatibility. The key to avoidance is to do your homework. Before you purchase anything, answer these questions: Which interface will my computer support—USB 1, 2 or Firewire? Do I need to upgrade via PCI/PCIe card? Which operating system am I running and which version (32 or 64 bit)? Are there other hardware considerations on my PC? Then, check the forums to see if other users are experiencing any problems with a like model computer and/or chipset. Once you have completed your homework, you can feel confident and informed in your purchase. To minimize compatibility issues, you should look for an audio device from a new retailer, rather than a used device from Craigslist or another used-gear source. Only if you've really done your homework and know for sure that the device you have chosen is compatible with your particular operating system should you buy a used device.

Depending on your PC, you may be stuck with USB as your only interface choice—not that that's a bad choice. Just make sure it's the right choice. What counts is that your audio device works with your machine, has the right number and type of connections you need to make the kind of recordings you want to make, is easy to use and sounds great.

Summing Up USB/Firewire Choices

- USB v1 devices offer slow-to-poor performance and are limited to 2 tracks of simultaneous recording.

- USB v1.1 devices can be "bus powered" by plugging them into your computer's USB port, or they may require an additional power adapter plugged into a power outlet.

- USB v2 allows recording of multiple audio tracks.

- USB v2 devices often require a separate power source, but some can be "bus powered" by plugging them into the computer's USB port.

- Audio interfaces often include MIDI inputs as a combo offering, and in that case, are usually available as Firewire or USB v2 devices.

- Firewire allows recording of multiple tracks.

- Some Firewire devices can be daisy-chained to increase the total number of simultaneous recording channels.

- Firewire devices can be both bus powered and powered by a power outlet, depending on the model and its feature set.

- Firewire offers two speed options: 400 and 800 Megabits per second. Each requires a different type of connector and unlike USB, they are not interchangeable with each other.

Checking Audio and MIDI Devices in Windows 7

After you have installed the necessary drivers and/or software per the instructions that came with your audio/MIDI device, it is simple to verify that your operating system "sees" your hardware. On Windows 7, you should see a box in the lower right-hand corner of the screen indicating that the hardware was installed correctly and is ready to use. You can double-check that Windows is recognizing your hardware and it is functioning correctly by opening the Device Manager and looking at the appropriate list item on the left. For audio devices, click on the triangle next to the "Sound, video and game controllers" item on the list. In the expanded menu below this item, you should see your audio device listed. After you locate the correct device, right-click on it and select "Properties." The window that opens will give you information about your audio device and let you know if it is working properly. This same procedure holds true for MIDI devices and combination audio/MIDI devices.

At this point, I recommend you turn off your default Windows sounds Fig. 7). It is inevitable that you will be working away with the volume turned up and inadvertently cause an error message to pop up, accompanied by a Windows sound blasting through your speakers. You'll end up turning off these sounds anyway once you have peeled yourself off the ceiling and cleaned up your coffee spill, so you might as well take the time to do that now.

It is an easy process: Click on the Sounds tab, found in the Sound Control Panel control. In the drop-down menu, choose "No Sounds." If you have customized your sounds, first click on "Save As" and name the sound set. This way, you can quickly restore those sounds when you are not working on an audio production.

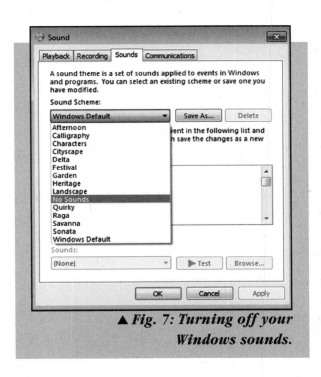

▲ *Fig. 7: Turning off your*
Windows sounds.

Routine PC Maintenance

It's important to perform routine maintenance on your PC from time to time. Files change and new files are continually added to hard drives, which can degrade performance over time. Defragmentation of your hard drive is a good routine procedure. To do this, go to Start>Programs>Accessories>System Tools and choose the Disk Defragmenter. This utility will analyze your disk and alert you if a defrag should be performed on your hard disk.

Other maintenance routines include keeping your Recycle Bin empty. This may seem elementary, but you'd be amazed how many times this task goes unchecked. Also, some audio systems are never connected to the internet except for critical downloads or registration; this virtually eliminates the need to run virus protection in the background. I am not telling you not to have virus protection, but I am saying is that if you are careful and intentional about using your audio system, you can avoid running virus software full-time. In this case, a better option would be to disable virus software and remove the computer from the internet while working on audio. All of these background processes, including Windows and other software updates, require system resources, which will limit available processing resources when working in Sonar.

I Can't See My Audio Device!

If you don't see your audio device listed, the problem is likely is due to one of the following reasons:

Likely Reasons You Can't See
Your Audio Device

- It is not plugged into your computer.

- It requires additional power to work and it's not plugged into the wall or not turned on.

- It does not have the necessary drivers installed.

- It is a problem caused by a combination of the above items.

I know these steps all sound too simple, but check them first if you don't see it. The same rules apply to your MIDI device. Sometimes you may need to restart your computer if it is acting wonky. And at other times, if your computer stops recognizing your audio or MIDI device, it can help to unplug them and plug them back in.

You should now have a rudimentary understanding of various audio and MIDI devices, their types of connections, and how to make sure your computer is seeing them. In our next chapter we'll move on to choosing and using microphones with Sonar.

CHAPTER 4 CHOOSING AND USING MICROPHONES

Technically, you *can* record with the microphone that comes built into your computer, but you'd be pretty unhappy with the results. The computer's internal mic is designed to capture your speaking voice for informal chats over the web etc. It is not designed to capture the subtle nuances of your high-end Taylor or vintage Gibson guitar, nor will it make you sound like Frank Sinatra or Norah Jones. If you have a great song idea and don't have time to set up the gear, you can certainly fire up your computer, set your input for the internal microphone and get your ideas down, but the sonic results will certainly be less than pleasing. Give it a try; you'll see what I mean.

For quality recording, you'll need a quality mic. Let's talk about basic microphone types, and how to choose the mic that will get the best results for your songs in Sonar. Microphones come in primarily three types:

MINI SONAR LESSON

Three Types of Microphones

- **Dynamic Microphones.** Dynamic microphones are typically used for live performances; they can be either hand-held or placed on a microphone stand.

- **Condenser Microphones.** Condenser microphones are commonly used in recording, broadcast media and similar applications. These mics typically require power from the mixer or another connected device in order to work.

- **Ribbon Microphones.** A ribbon mic is a type of dynamic microphone that suspends a thin aluminum, duraluminum or nanofilm ribbon between the poles of a magnet to generate voltage variations through electromagnetic induction.

Dynamic Microphones

A dynamic, or moving-coil microphone captures sound and converts it to electrical information by acting as a tiny loudspeaker wired in reverse. Sound is captured by a diaphragm, which is surrounded by a movable induction coil, positioned in the magnetic field of a permanent magnet. Sound moves the diaphragm, which causes it to vibrate, and in turn, the coil in the magnetic field moves. This action produces varying current through electromagnetic induction. If you unscrew the round windscreen cover from, say, a Shure SM58 or SM57, you'll see what looks like a little speaker inside. And that's exactly what a mic is, a little speaker—only it's wired backward.

Dynamic mics are available in a variety of sound pick-up patterns ranging from unidirectional, meaning they pick up sound from one direction, to omnidirectional, meaning they pick up sound from everywhere.

Dynamic microphones don't require power to operate. You can simply plug them into their cables, connect them to your mixer or device, set the level and you're good to go.

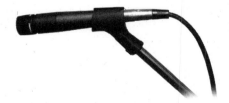
Fig. 8a: Dynamic microphone

Condenser Microphones

Condenser microphones work differently than dynamic microphones: Here, the diaphragm serves as one plate of a capacitor or "capsule," which is made up of one fixed plate and one movable plate. Sound vibrations produce variations in the distance between the capacitor's plates, generating voltage differences.

Condenser microphones require power to work. Professional microphones typically use XLR-connector cables; the power for condenser mics comes down the XLR cable or through a battery installed in the mic itself. Most of the time, condensers are powered by phantom power, a means for sending electrical current through a microphone cable to operate microphones containing active electronic circuitry. Phantom power is commonly built into mixers of all sizes, from the smallest to the largest, and is found in microphone preamplifiers and other audio equipment such as digital recording interfaces for computers. Phantom power can also directly or indirectly supply the voltage used for polarizing the microphone's capsule.

If phantom power is not engaged, the microphone won't function. It's the first thing to check when you're setting levels, and when you push that power button, always turn down your headphone or speaker volume, as well as the microphone channel level. Some better condenser microphones, especially those that are powered by vacuum tubes, come with their own power supply.

Fig. 8b: Condensor microphone

In some cases, the microphone might have a 9-volt battery or an internal battery that recharges itself while connected to a power source. This isn't very common, but I do own some microphones that feature batteries, such as the Rode NT3, which can house a 9-volt battery, or the CAD Equitek E-100, which contains a rechargeable battery. These configurations allow me to use these microphones in the rare situations where I am not able to power them from the mixer or recording device.

Condenser microphones can be unidirectional, meaning they are intended to pick up sound primarily from one side of the microphone. They can also be bidirectional, meaning they pick up sound from both sides; this pattern is usually controlled by a switch on the microphone. These mics sometimes come with a rotating switch that lets you change the mic's pickup pattern from a single unidirectional side to a figure-8 pattern, which picks up sounds from both sides of the capsule. Using this pattern can open up the sound of your voice, or pick up a guitar or other instrument in a whole new way that you may find appealing. Play around with the settings—and when you find one that sounds right, it *is* right!

I've purposely left out a lot of the techno-babble that you probably don't care about right now. My goal is to give you a basic understanding of microphones so you can make the right choice to record with Sonar.

Ribbon Microphones

A ribbon microphone is a type of dynamic microphone that suspends a thin aluminum, duraluminum or nanofilm ribbon between the poles of a magnet to generate voltage varations through electromagnetic induction. Sound energy causes this ribbon to move, and an electrical current is induced. Ribbon microphones are typically bidirectional, meaning they pick up sounds equally well from either side of the microphone.

Ribbon mics are somewhat fragile, so treat them very carefully. If you're interested in building up a nice mic collection, you'll want an affordable ribbon mic in the mix, but I wouldn't recommend it as your sole microphone.

Choosing a Microphone that Matches Your Needs

Why would you use a condenser microphone for recording, when a dynamic works great for live concert performances? It's really all about the power and frequency range of your source material, and the range and sensitivity of dynamic microphones versus condenser mics. If you have access to dynamics, ribbons and condensers, you should try all three on various sources and hear for yourself how each mic "sounds" on a wide variety of sources. Also, keep in mind that dynamics and most ribbons do not require phantom power to operate, so their applications are more flexible—such as, with the right adapter, plugging directly into a computer's microphone input.

A condenser mic, unless it has an internal battery, cannot be connected with an adapter to your computer like the dynamic mic can, but in any event, steer clear of plugging anything directly into your computer's microphone input if you can; your audio interface will provide the necessary phantom power for your condenser microphone.

The best advice is to try different types of microphones and listen to the sonic signature of each, to learn which ones sound great for your voice, or for your guitar or other instruments.

Cost need not be an issue. You can get some pretty decent microphones for home recording for under $100 these days, and for a few hundred dollars, you can get a professional-quality microphone that rivals the sound of those costing much more. The trick is to find a pro audio retailer who will let you put on some headphones and get into a space where you can sing into a variety of mics without much outside interference, so you can determine the perfect microphone before you purchase it. If they can't do that, make sure they have a liberal return policy so you can try out the microphone at home. A microphone choice is a very personal decision, almost like finding the right pair of shoes to fit your feet.

▲ *Fig. 8c: Ribbon microphone.*

You can buy some pretty nice USB condenser microphones, which actually get their power from USB, so they act as a combination microphone and audio interface in one. If you're only going to record one track at a time, it's very easy to justify owning only one decent-sounding USB microphone plugged into your PC alongside one USB-powered MIDI keyboard. However, this approach does not leave you with much flexibility.

USB microphones are marketed primarily to people who do voiceover recording or capture single-input audio (such as a reporters, field recorders or podcasters) and need maximum portability for recording direct to a notebook computer. If I had written this book a year ago, I would have advised against USB microphones, but now, good options are available from reputable companies. If a USB microphone's single-channel recording limitation is acceptable, go for it.

▲ *Fig. 8d: USB microphone*

In summary, your basic recording rig should include a USB or Firewire audio interface that includes at least 2 channels (works with your operating system and offers 48-volt phantom power), a pair of microphones that are as good as your budget will allow, and a USB MIDI keyboard. For monitoring, add some good speakers and quality headphones. (Don't skimp here; you get what you pay for!) These basic tools, coupled with a powerful computer running Sonar, will allow you to create awesome recordings.

If you want to delve deeper into microphones, I highly suggest reading *Professional Microphone Techniques* by David Miles Huber and Philip Williams (ArtistPro Publishing, 1999). You'll learn more about the workings of all types of microphones, as well as technique for placing mics on instruments. You can also listen to audio examples on the book's accompanying CD.

CHAPTER 5 — SETTING UP YOUR FIRST PROJECT IN SONAR

It's time to get ready to record in Sonar–but first, you'll need to install and register the software. Before installing Sonar, install the appropriate drivers for your audio and MIDI interfaces and confirm that the installation was successful. You should also go through any testing procedures that your hardware manufacturer recommends. The Sonar box includes a serial number; protect this number and keep it somewhere safe. There will likely come a time when you have to reinstall the software or need this number for an upgrade. I will usually type it in a text document and save that to the Documents folder of my audio computer.

If you've completed these steps, you're ready to move on to the installation DVD.

Upon inserting the DVD, an interactive program should start automatically. If it doesn't, manually launch the interactive start screen by double-clicking the DVD drive and clicking the Setup icon. (Note that the program DVD also contains documentation and utilities.) Generally, I will let Sonar install all of its files in the default directories. I set up another partition for all virtual instruments (VST) program files, because I use multiple audio software titles (although Sonar is my favorite, really!) and I like to have all VSTs in one place for easier management. Let Sonar put a shortcut on your desktop for easy access. After you have installed the software, restart your computer.

Depending on the version of Sonar you purchased, your package may include additional disks featuring all sorts of goodies from free VST plug-ins to utilities and demos of other software. I recommend installing them and trying them out when you're ready. If you don't like them, you can always uninstall.

Physical Connections

To help ensure that everything runs smoothly, take your time configuring physical connections between your audio interface, MIDI interface, microphones, speakers, headphones, MIDI controllers and other studio peripherals. For this example, I will keep everything pretty simple and basic.

Let's start with audio. The first thing you need to do is make sure your audio interface is turned on and correctly connected to the computer. Then, using an XLR mic cable, plug the female end into your mic and the male end into channel 1 on your audio interface. If you are using a condenser mic, make sure you have 48-volt phantom power turned on for that channel. Plug your audio interface's analog output 1 into your left speaker and analog output 2 into your right speaker. Make sure your speakers are turned on! If your interface has a dedicated headphone output, plug in your headphones now.

Now for physical MIDI connections. I'll assume you have a dedicated USB MIDI interface and a MIDI keyboard controller. You should have already completed the installation procedure for your interface. For this example, you only need to make two connections: one from your keyboard to your interface, and a second one from your interface to your computer. Plug one end of a MIDI cable into the controller's MIDI Out jack and the other end of the MIDI cable into your interface's MIDI In port. Then plug your MIDI interface into your computer and power it on.

Fire It Up!

Launch Sonar by double-clicking the icon on your desktop. On the first launch, you will be prompted to register. To do so, just follow the instructions on the screen. If you use your program menu, Sonar will appear in the Cakewalk folder. You will see the window shown on the right (Fig. 9).

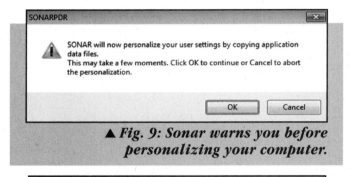

▲ *Fig. 9: Sonar warns you before personalizing your computer.*

Click OK and let Sonar do its thing.

Sonar will then prompt you with another window. This window will conduct a series of tests on your audio and MIDI hardware. Make sure that your hardware is on and ready and press OK. Take the time to run this test; in fact, run this test any time you encounter trouble with your audio interfaces to help verify that Sonar recognizes and is playing nicely with the audio devices (Fig. 10). (You can also run this test within Sonar; I'll go over that process in a bit.)

When this test is complete, a new window will display compatible sampling and bit rates for your hardware.

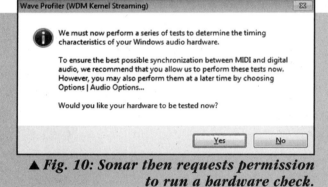

▲ *Fig. 10: Sonar then requests permission to run a hardware check.*

After the software has loaded, a dialog box will ask how you want to proceed: open a recent project, new project, etc. Choose "Create a New Project." You will be asked whether you want to open one of the many templates that come with Sonar, or open a blank project. Choose "Blank Project" (Fig. 11).

The next dialog box will ask you to name your project and choose a location for it. I highly recommend that you store your audio sessions and recordings on a separate, dedicated hard drive, not your system/OS drive. It's also a good idea to keep your VST sample libraries on still another dedicated hard drive. By storing these files on their own dedicated drives, your entire system will run more smoothly and get much better performance! Worst case, get an external drive and back up often.

▲ *Fig. 11: A dialog box asks you how to proceed.*

Choose a location for our test project by navigating to your dedicated audio recording hard drive. Create a new folder on your audio drive and name it "test." Name the project "test" as well.

Speaking of file names and recording paths, let me tell you a story about one person's nightmare, which I had the pleasure of trying to sort out. One day I got a phone call from "Johnny." Johnny was in a state of panic because his system drive only had 2 MB of available space, and he couldn't save the project he was working on. He didn't know why his main system drive was so full; he had a dedicated audio drive that had plenty of available space. I told him to look for large files or folders. He located an audio folder on his system drive that was more than 30 gigabytes in size! I asked him if he had been saving his projects to his audio drive; he assured me that all of his projects were on that dedicated drive. He opened the audio drive and said, "Yep, I see all the songs I've been working on. They are all here." Well, I knew that something was drastically amiss. I told him to open that 30-gig audio folder on his system drive and tell me what he saw. He said that there were about 50 files named "audio 1," 50 more named "audio 2," and so on. To make a long story short, he had originally saved his first project to his system drive, made a few test recordings and set up a template. That meant that all of his audio files were recorded on his system drive. At some point, someone told him that he should move his projects to his audio drive instead. So, he just copied the project file from his system drive to his audio drive. Then, every subsequent project he started originated from this project file; all of the audio files were still being recorded to the system drive because he never changed the recording path for new songs. He just kept opening that original Sonar file and saving it as a new song name on his audio drive—but the files were still being written to the system drive.

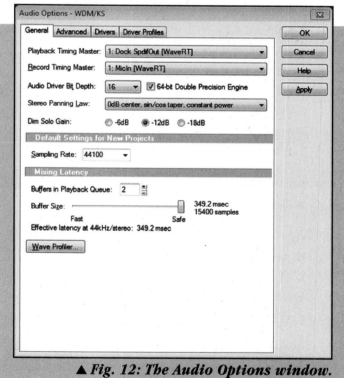

▲ *Fig. 12: The Audio Options window.*

I'm sharing this story just to illustrate the importance of understanding your file structure and knowing where things are written to disk. Johnny was not careful about naming his tracks or establishing a proper folder structure before he recorded, so he had a major mess on his hands.

Now that we've created a test project, we need to make sure that Sonar is "seeing" our audio and MIDI hardware: Click on the menu title Options>Audio, to open the window to all things audio (Fig. 12).

Here, you will choose the correct audio device, bit rate and latency. CDs store 44.1kHz/16-bit audio; most professional recording studios use a higher sampling and bit rate and dither the audio down to the CD rate when mastering, but this decision is totally up to you. Generally, a higher sampling/bit rate will provide better fidelity, but larger files require more processing power and hard drive space.

Latency

Latency is the delay introduced by the amount of time it takes for an analog signal to travel through a microphone into an audio interface, convert to a digital signal, process through Sonar, convert from digital back to analog and travel into your ears. That sounds like a very time-consuming process, but today's interfaces and computers process information so quickly that this delay can be virtually undetectable. Both Sonar and your audio interface let you control, to a certain degree, the amount of latency present while you are recording. Why does this matter? If you're playing music, if there is a lot of latency, your performance will suffer; your timing will be off because when you play a note, you will hear a noticeable delay. In addition, latency affects responsiveness of mixing controls. However, as you lower latency, you increase CPU load.

Sonar's Audio Options window features a Mixing Latency slider, which lets you adjust your buffer size, which determines the audio delay after that trip through your system. The lower the setting, the lower the latency; the higher the number is set, the higher the latency. When recording, you should always set this parameter as low as you can and still have your system perform reliably. Your computer will be working much harder at lower buffer settings than at higher ones, however, so if you don't need to have lower latency, i.e. when you are mixing, a higher buffer setting will give you more processing power (Fig. 13).

▲ *Fig. 13: The Mixing Latency slider in the Audio Options window.*

One other note on this window: Below the Latency section, you'll find a button labeled Wave Profiler. Remember when we first opened Sonar and it performed a series of tests on our audio sound card? Well, this is that button. If you change hardware or tweak settings and are having trouble, run this Wave profiler again. It's the first step in troubleshooting communication between hardware and software.

Back in the Audio Options window, I want to highlight two settings under the Advanced tab. Driver Mode will generally be set to ASIO. If you are unsure of your device settings, check the specifications on the sound card to see what the manufacturer recommends. I'd also like to point out the Caching setting. Cache this spot in your memory because if you have problems on playback or recording, depending on your computer setup, it may be necessary to come back to this window and enable both Read Caching and Write Caching. Read and Write Caching functions use your internal hard disk as a temporary storage device if the hard disk cannot keep up with delivering the audio as requested. This is usually only evident if you have an older disk controller. Depending on your computer's age and hardware configuration, enabling caching may improve your system's performance.

Naming Your Device

Click on the Drivers tab in the Audio Options window. The input and output devices you see enabled here are the available inputs/outputs within Sonar. Take a moment and give these inputs friendly names, like I did in the screen below. Check the items you want to have available and then double-click the name to rename. Strategic naming helps you stay organized if you have multiple inputs or outputs that are consistently routed to one thing. For instance, if Channel 1 is always hooked up to your favorite microphone, you could name that input "My Mic." The more you think this through on the front end, the easier everything will be when the creativity is flowing.

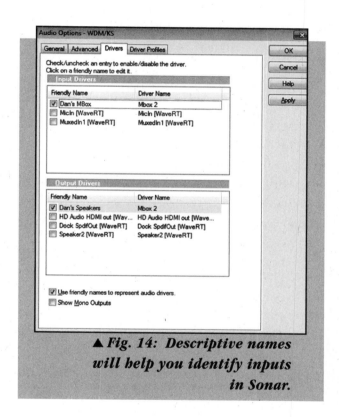

▲ *Fig. 14: Descriptive names will help you identify inputs in Sonar.*

On to Making Music

By now you're well on your way to start using Sonar. You have a solid foundation of knowledge about finding the right devices, choosing microphones, setting up your system and creating your first project file for your first recording session. In the next chapter, we'll take a look at recording MIDI and audio tracks.

WORKING WITH LOOPS

CHAPTER
6

Now that we've talked about connecting your audio and MIDI devices, choosing a microphone and configuring your basic project settings in Sonar, it's time to make some music. We'll start by getting familiar with some basic loop handling. Loops are audio phrases or measures that have been designed to be repeated without losing time; their tempo and pitch can be adjusted to fit your recording. A loop's flexibility will depend on how far you are trying to stretch it. For example, a 140 bpm drum loop will probably not sound good at 80 bpm. The benefit to loops is they can provide instant creativity and inspiration. If you have a good rhythm idea but you don't have a drummer, it may be useful to find a good loop to help communicate what you are hearing and feeling for the song. Loops are not limited to drums; they are available for every instrument and sound.

Welcoming Loops Into Your Session

Prerecorded audio loops are available from a variety of sources; sites sell loop disks and downloads for purchase, and some creative surfing even can land you some free ones. Once you've collected some loops, it is time to review and import. In the File Menu, choose Import Audio to locate the desired loop on your hard drive. Another way that Sonar manages Loop auditioning, management and importing is through the Media Browser (formerly named the Loop Explorer). To open the Media Browser, either click on the icon [icon] or select the Views menu, then choose the Media Browser.

Once you open the Media Browser, navigate to your loop location. On my system, I dedicated a folder on my audio drive named—you guessed it—Loops. I store all of my loops in this folder so I can easily access them. At the top of the browser, you will see a box labeled Content Location. If you find yourself returning to the same location again and again, or you have a group of favorite loops that you're regularly pulling from, then navigate to that folder, put in a title in the Content Location and press the Save button. Next time you open the Media Browser, just click on the down arrow and your saved locations will be listed.

Sonar Shortcuts

On any Menu, to the right of the menu items you will see a series of keystrokes and a number. These are shortcuts to launch tasks. For example, to launch the Media Browser, normally accessed in the View menu, click Alt + 1. These shortcuts are a great way to quickly navigate common tasks without having to use the mouse.

▲ *Fig. 15: Look to the right of each menu item to find the shortcut for that item.*

The Media Browser is useful for auditioning and inserting much more than audio loops. I'll give you a quick overview; when you're ready to dig in further, I recommend reading the Media Browser chapter in the Sonar manual.

To audition a loop, click on the loop once to select it, and then click the Audition play button. Or, press the Auto play button, which will automatically start playing the selected loop (Fig. 16). The loop will automatically play at the tempo of your project so you can tell right away if it will fit in your project. Once you find a loop with the correct feel, and it still works well when you adjust its tempo to match the song's tempo, double-click on the loop name and it automatically loads into the session at the cursor position on the selected track. It's okay if the loop doesn't line up perfectly; you can slide it around to find that perfect spot. Take note! I am about to share with you the most important shortcut to know when you are working in Sonar. Ready? Ctrl Z=undo! This function will continue to come in handy as you make your way around the workstation.

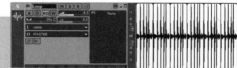

▲ *Fig. 16: The Media Browser tool bar includes Play, Stop and Auto Play functions.*

Once you load the loop into the session, press Alt-0, which is the shortcut for the Track View, and you will be back at the main recording/editing window.

When a loop is imported into your session, it is also copied into your session folder. This helps keep your session elements together in the same folder, which makes for ease of transport if you need to access the files for any reason, or you take the session to another computer.

Once a loop is imported into your Track View, you can make adjustments to it. Right-click on the loop and choose Clip Properties. You'll see three tabs, but the middle tab is where I want to focus. Here, you can choose from two clip types: Groove Clip and Audio Snap. In the case of loops, we will be selecting Groove Clip with Enable Looping Checked. My test loop has 8 beats in a clip: Changing this number to 4 will double-time the loop; changing it to 16 will half time the loop. There will be a point where every loop starts to sound unnatural if it is stretched too far, but there are times when that effect may be just what you are looking for.

Where Groove Clip will enable you to treat a clip as a loop, Audio Snap analyzes the transients of a loop for further manipulation. This would apply, for instance, if you have a loop or even a recorded drum track that you would like to quantize or adjust to match the session's tempo or adjust the session to follow the tempo of the clip. (Audio Snap is more like surgery of the clip, where Groove Clip is adjusting the existing clip.) For basic manipulation of imported loops, Groove Clip should do the trick. The beauty of loops is they can be dragged and expanded, lengthening the loop's duration. To adjust a loop's length, mouse over the middle of the loop and the beginning or end of the loop and you will see the tool turn into a small box with a two-way arrow. Now, click-and-drag on the end of the loop to expand or contract the loop. The loop's beginning point will show a small notch at the top; this is a visual indicator of the loop's length and it's a quick way to identify how many times the loop has been used (Fig. 17).

▲ *Fig. 17: A loop that has been repeated five times, as indicated by the number of notches shown at the top of the waveform.*

CHAPTER 7 RECORDING AND EDITING AUDIO

Navigating the Session

Before we start routing audio and MIDI, we need to take a look at the Large Transport Bar (Fig. 18), the central point for navigation within Sonar. The standard Transport Bar is embedded

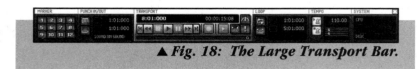

▲ *Fig. 18: The Large Transport Bar.*

in the default tools at the top of the Sonar Screen. The Large Transport Bar is a floating window that encompasses the most common functions needed to navigate a session, including time, tempo, metronome, markers and standard transport functions. The Transport Bar can be viewed by clicking the F4 function key, a shortcut that toggles between showing and hiding the Transport Bar. The controls found this section can also be accessed individually on the toolbar at the top of the Sonar session window, but for the majority of our work here, the Large Transport window will suffice. To view and customize this toolbar, right-click on it to see a list of options (Fig. 19).

The Large Transport is broken down into six primary sections: Marker, Punch In/Out, Transport, Loop, Tempo and System. I'll focus on two sections: Transport and Tempo. The Transport section is similar to transports found on every CD and tape player–and even 8-tracks, if you want to go really retro–with a few additions. One function that works a little differently is the Record button (indicated by an O on the button). Arming a track readies that track for recording; however, to actually begin recording, you must press the Record button on the transport. When I was first starting out, I would arm the track and hit Play, and everything appeared to be recording, but nothing actually was recorded. It was because I did not press the Record button on the transport! We'll explore this more in a bit.

The Tempo section lets you define the default tempo for the song. Establish tempo first, before you ever start recording or importing loops. Define the song's meter and key signature by clicking on the small music staff. The buttons on the left configure a click track, which we will explore in more detail. (If any button is unclear, mouse over the button to see a description of the button's function.)

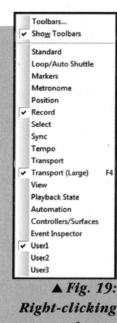

▲ *Fig. 19: Right-clicking on the top toolbar in the Sonar session will prompt you with a list of available tools to customize your toolbar.*

Recording Audio

When I create a new project, whether I am writing something from scratch or producing a big Nashville recording session, I always start by defining the tempo. Even if I decide to change it later, it is a good idea to set the tempo as a starting point. The easiest way to decide on a tempo is to turn on the click track by clicking the Click button on the Transport panel and pressing the spacebar. The default tempo for a new project is 120 beats per minute. While the transport is running, you can manually type in tempo values in the Tempo field on the Transport panel. Use the Tempo view if you plan on programming tempo and/or meter changes in your song; Otherwise, the Fixed Tempo option is probably a better choice.

Next, create as many audio tracks as you need for your recording session. If you only have a 2-channel audio interface but you know you are going to be recording 4 guitar tracks and 4 vocals, you may want to create 8 audio tracks. Sonar will create stereo tracks by default, but when you assign inputs to those tracks, Sonar will set the track to mono if you're only using one input.

In your new blank Sonar project, if you chose the blank template when starting, you won't have any tracks. The Insert Menu gives you three options for adding tracks: Audio, MIDI and Multiple Tracks. For our test project, choose Multiple Tracks and set the Audio tracks to 8 and MIDI tracks to 1. Click OK, and the tracks will be created for you (Fig. 20).

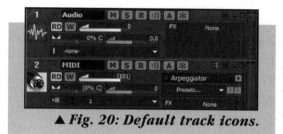

▲ *Fig. 20: Default track icons.*

Each type of track has a default image associated with it. As you can see from the image, the audio track image is a sound wave and the MIDI track displays a MIDI connector. These pictures can be changed, but for now I want to point out the default images, which can be helpful when navigating a full Sonar session.

When you insert a track (or tracks) it will be placed by default below the last track in the session. Alternatively, if you right-click on a track and choose Insert Track, new tracks will be inserted immediately above that track. Each track has a series of buttons below the track name; by dragging the bottom of the track, you can adjust the window to display more of the basic controls.

To record, set the Input to the active input (where your instrument or microphone is plugged in). Earlier I talked about giving your sound card inputs "friendly" names by navigating to the Options menu>Audio, then the Drivers tabs. When you set your track input, a list of available inputs will appear. This is where these descriptive names can be a big help.

After you select input, click on the R button, which will record-enable the input. Now it's time to make some noise; while adjusting the input gain on your sound card, you should see the meter on that track light up with the sound of your voice or instrument sent to the track. When setting inputs be sure to watch the level both on your sound card input and on the meter within Sonar. In the world of digital recording, signal entering into the red area on the meter equals distortion, which equals an unhappy engineer and performer.

The Track Pane (viewable within the Track View) contains all of the necessary controls for setting input, output and recording (Fig. 21). The larger view to the left provides an overview of everything associated with a given track, including input, EQ, inserts and fader; this window will change, depending which track is selected.

Before we move ahead, let's review the steps to add an audio track to your Sonar project and prepare to record your microphone or electronic instrument input:

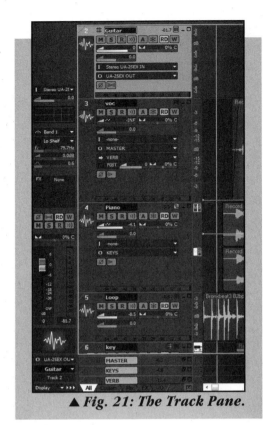

▲ *Fig. 21: The Track Pane.*

Adding an Audio Track to Your Project

1. Choose an input from the Insert menu, or right-click on the Track view and choose Insert Track.

2. Set your input on the track from the drop-down menu under the Record button.

3. Arm the track by pressing the R button.

4. Make some noise while adjusting the level on your sound card to confirm the level is present in your session.

5. Turn up your monitors to verify that the signal is coming through the system. By default, new tracks are set to the default output.

Name It, Now!

One more thing about adding new tracks: You really need to label your tracks with descriptive names. If you do not give each track a name, it will get confusing trying to remember what is on each track if they are all called "Track ##," which is the default label for new audio tracks.

VST (Virtual Studio Technology, an interface technology for integrating virtual instruments, synths or effects with workstations) tracks are assigned a default name for the instrument being played, but you can rename them, as well. This is especially helpful if you've created a special part on a track that you'll remember more easily if it has a unique name.

Label the track by double-clicking the track name to highlight it so it allows you to type in a new name for it. Labeling is a very important part of the production process; be sure to get in the habit of labeling your tracks as soon as each one is created.

Eight Key Track Functions

MIDI and audio tracks use the same simple controls. Under the name of each track, you'll see eight buttons. I'll take you through the function of each.

The first button mutes or un-mutes the track, letting you choose whether or not you hear the track in the mix. For example, if you have recorded a bunch of tracks and want to hear what they sound like with the background vocal removed, just hit the mute button on that track to turn it off.

The second button solos the track. In other words, when you play your mix and tracks are soloed, you will only hear those tracks; all other tracks are muted.

The third button arms the track for recording. Red means that track is ready to record and gray means recording is disabled on that track.

The fourth button turns monitoring on and off, which we'll discuss in detail later in this chapter.

The fifth button sets the track to Archive, which is a hard mute that cannot be overwritten with the global Mute button (the red/yellow M at the bottom of the track view)

The sixth button freezes the track, which bounces the audio in the track to a new audio clip or clips, applies effects, and disables the FX bin. Any plug-ins inserted into a track are stored in this bin; as more and more plug-ins are added, they become more taxing on your computer. Freezing creates a nondestructive copy of that track with the effects applied and bypasses the entire FX bin, which frees up the processing resources that those FX were using. This configuration is easily undone by clicking the Freeze button again. The Freeze function's purpose is to free up system resources.

Freezing a Software Instrument track also saves the track as an audio file in the project. This is a good idea to turn on as soon as you are certain that your part is exactly as you want it to be. Software instrument tracks require a lot of computer processing power, so converting the MIDI data's triggered part from a software instrument takes the pressure off of the processors.

This function is also useful for Audio tracks with complex effects, which also eat up a lot of your processing power. If you find that Sonar is stopping during playback and indicating that it's running out of steam, freeze the tracks that are using a large number of effects. Remember, freezing a track isn't permanent. If you want to make changes later, you can unlock the track, make the changes, and then freeze the track again.

The seventh and eighth buttons relate to automation, and work together. RD stands for Read Automation—as in, playing back automation that has been written to the track. If this button is not enabled, automation on that track will be ignored. W stands for Write, as in writing new automation, and will enable the track's automation to go into Record mode. In simple terms, automation is a process that automatically controls an element of the track. It could be that you'd like to automatically fade the volume of the track in or out during a section of your song; or maybe you want Sonar to automatically pan the sound of your groovy tambourine part from left to right during part of the song.

Envelopes are "shapes" for any elements that can be automated on that track; right-clicking in a track's wave view will give you the option of inserting envelopes. You will always see volume and pan (left-right placement) functions, but additional envelopes may be available, depending on what kind of processing (effects, EQ, etc.) is enabled on that track. To create an envelope, enable the type of envelope you want to apply, and double-click on the line that appears on the track. You can drag this point up and down to create a curve; continue adding dots and moving them around to shape the volume curve of the entire track. You can add as many dots as you want and drag them up and down to set volume, panning or effects. That's automation, in a nutshell.

Recording Test Audio

At this point we have inserted a track, configured the input to correspond with the input that we plugged our instrument or microphone into. Arm the track, and if everything has been set correctly, you will see audio show up on the track meter within Sonar. If you are recording a mono (single-channel) track, you may see only the left or right meter displaying a signal. This is because the track input is set to a stereo pair of inputs. This is an easy fix: Click on the track's Input section, scroll down to your sound card, and choose either the Left or Right input. This option may vary depending on how your sound card is listed, but the key is to tell it that you are recording a mono signal. The meter will now reflect a mono track and you should see signal appearing in the entire meter area.

Recording Audio, For Real

You've now created and armed a track, routed audio, established tempo and possibly imported a loop. Now let's record something for real. But first, if you chose a loop in conjunction with or instead of the click track, be sure to lay it out on your track to match the arrangement of the material you are recording. You can add virtually as many loops as you want. If you want the same loop at a different points in the track, you can click on the loop to select it, copy it and choose the elements you want to copy. For this instance, we will only copy the Events, which means the loop itself; the other options do not apply to this session. Move the timeline to the spot where you want to insert the loop and paste it in.

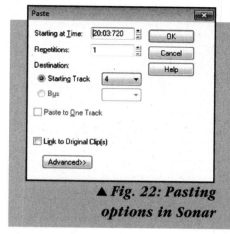

▲ *Fig. 22: Pasting options in Sonar*

When you paste a loop, you will be prompted with a window (Fig. 22). This will allow you to set the start time, number of repetitions and selected track, and choose whether you want to link the loop to the original clip.

Look for the metronome in the Tempo section of the Transport window. You have three metronome options: You can set it to play only during recording, only during playback, or both.

Now, the loop and/or metronome is ready. Make sure the track is armed, then click the Record button on the transport. The track is now in Record mode, and you can begin the process of recording your masterpiece. One of the great benefits of digital recording is the fact that it is nondestructive, which means that your actions do not affect the original file; rather, you are recording a set of actions that you can modify. In general, your original recorded audio will remain intact on your hard drive unless you intentionally record over it or delete it manually. Let's focus on choosing how we record over previous audio.

Let's say, like on the DVD where Jessica is recording her vocal track, the overall recording was pretty good, but you'd like to re-record one section. You do not have to start over again from the beginning; instead, you're going to "punch in" the new material.

Punching in and out, which is controlled in the Large Transport window, means playing along with the already recorded audio, punching in to record new audio, and then punching out to stop the track from recording and send it back to playing the previously recorded audio. This is called Sound on Sound mode in Sonar. Sound on Sound mode keeps the previous recording and adds another layer of recording onto that same track. This will allow you to go back later and use parts of different recordings to make one final track. It is also good for keeping the flow of the session moving for the artist. I prefer to set Sound on Sound mode and let the artist record multiple takes, one after the other. Then we can go back and listen to what was recorded and tweak from there. The other mode is called Overwrite. Overwrite means just that. It will overwrite what was previously recorded. This is destructive editing. Generally, I will work in Sound on Sound mode and edit out what I don't want. This is the safest method of recording (Fig. 23).

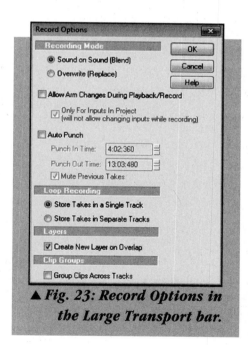

▲ *Fig. 23: Record Options in the Large Transport bar.*

I highly recommend working with these settings to get a feel for how each one works. Generally, I will work in Sound on Sound mode, set my punch in and out times and enable Mute Previous Takes so I don't hear what was recorded on the spot I am re-recording.

We'll tackle track editing in Chapter 8, but for now, continue punching in and out until that track has a performance you are ecstatic about. Repeat until satisfied.

You Did It!

Now you know how to create a new audio track and configure Sonar's inputs for your microphone, guitar or other instrument input. The next step is to start editing.

Editing in Sonar

Once recording is complete, editing begins. The amount of editing you do often depends on how well your material was recorded. If you were careful about punches, took the time to get things just right while recording and documented the takes well, editing may be quick. Often, however, recording means simply getting the take and moving on to the next take to keep the flow going.

Editing includes cross-fading files, cleaning up unwanted track noise and comping, which means compiling pieces of multiple takes together to create one outstanding track.

Working with Layers

If you record multiple takes of a track, Sonar places each take in a layer within the track. To view the layers on a track, click the Track Layers button, which is located to the immediate right of the track name in the track pane (Fig. 24).

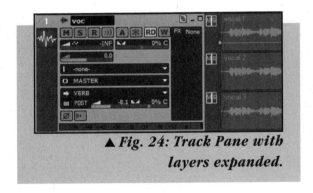

▲ *Fig. 24: Track Pane with layers expanded.*

Let's try editing vocals, using the best elements from the three takes to create one master vocal track. Start by muting all of the layers except for the top one, listen to it, and work your way down through the tracks. Take notes on the performance elements you like in each layer as you repeat the process, listening to all of the layers. The next step is cleaning up the takes on each layer and then blending them together. Let's say you like the first phrase on layer 1, second phrase on layer 3 and the final phrase on layer 2. Switch over to the zoom tool by pressing the Z key and draw a box around the layers you want to edit. This precision zoom will give you a detailed view of the edit points. Moving the Select tool to the edge of the take will change the tool into a resizing tool. A blue hue will appear at the edge of the clip; click on the edge of the clip to drag it to the point where you want that clip to begin. Repeat this process for the end of that clip and the other clips you want to adjust. If you place that same select tool on the upper corner of each of these clips, the tool changes and you will see a red hue appear; this is the fade tool. By clicking and dragging this tool toward the middle of the clip, you will see a line indicating the fade. Repeat this with each clip to assure they sound smooth when you play through all of them. If you pull a clip over the edge of another clip, you will be able to create and modify a crossfade, which fades on clip out as another is fading in. Crossfades can be handy when you are having trouble blending clips together. Finally, select the clips you're not using right now. Instead of deleting them, mute them by selecting and pressing Q.

Now, listen to the clips. Continue tweaking the edits until you get them just how you want them to sound. Once you're satisfied, select the clips, right-click and choose Bounce to Clips. This function will create one edited track, applying edits and fades removing muted tracks. Continue this process with all audio tracks containing layers.

Quick Editing Tips

- By holding down Shift while clicking on a clip, you can drag that clip across layers and/or tracks while preserving the clip's start time.

- Holding down Ctrl while clicking on a clip lets you to drag a copy of that clip to another layer or track.

- To split a clip, select the clip at the point of the split and press S.

- Right-click on a vocal clip and choose V-Vocal>Create V-Vocal Clip to open Sonar's vocal tuning utility (Fig. 25). This function is nondestructive and undoable; it's optimal to apply after the vocal is comped.

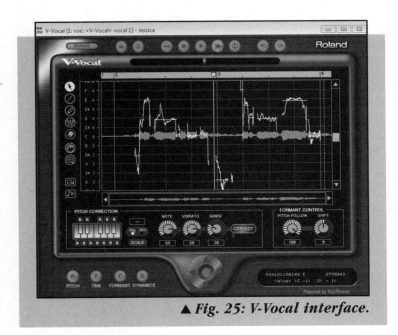

▲ *Fig. 25: V-Vocal interface.*

15 Things You Now Know About Sonar!

You've now learned the basics of setting up Sonar and recording audio. Let's review some key points before moving ahead with more in-depth work.

1. It's important to understand how your PC's firepower compares to Sonar's system requirements.

2. It is possible to record using your PC's own built-in audio inputs and outputs, but it isn't a good choice for serious recording projects.

3. The USB 1.1 spec is limited to two outputs for recording into Sonar, no matter how many inputs the device might have.

4. USB v2 audio devices are able to support more than two simultaneous outputs for recording.

5. Firewire audio devices are able to support more than two simultaneous outputs for recording.

6. Audio and MIDI devices can be either "bus" powered, receiving power directly from the USB or Firewire port, or powered from an electrical outlet, and sometimes can function both ways.

7. Condenser microphones are the best choice for recording and they require phantom power or battery power.

8. To add a track in Sonar, right-click on a track in the Edit window and choose Insert Audio/MIDI Track, or choose the track type in the Insert menu. You can also insert multiple tracks using this method.

9. Name your tracks as soon as you create them to avoid confusion later when mixing your project.

10. Each track offers eight key functions: Mute, Solo, Record, Input Monitor, Archive, Freeze Track and Automate Read/Write.

11. The round Record button on the Transport bar activates recording for any track that shows the R button selected. Red means ready to record.

12. The track view within the Edit Window lets you adjust a variety of track settings, from inputs, to monitoring the sound, to setting the input recording level. You can also add effects, change your software instrument or set other customizing features.

13. To rehearse your parts, turn on Monitoring to play or sing along with your tracks before recording, but turn monitoring off when you're done practicing to avoid a feedback loop.

14. Latency is the amount of delay introduced by the time it takes your audio to pass through the system. If you hit a note or sing a word and hear a noticeable delay, then lower your latency. Latency performance is affected by the number of active plug-ins and virtual instruments, as well as the available system processing.

15. Multiple recordings on the same track are stored as layers. Layers can be used to comp different takes together into one seamless clip.

If you've learned these functions and followed these steps, you're ready to start putting your hit down in a new recording session. But there's a lot more to learn about using Sonar, so keep reading; next, we'll talk about using MIDI to really soup up your recording sessions.

RECORDING AND EDITING MIDI

Now that you have an understanding of working with audio in Sonar, it is time to jump into MIDI (Musical Instrument Digital Interface). Sonar's MIDI capabilities are vast and extensive! Rather than discuss them all in great detail, I'll show you a few things to get you going and start the creative process. Once you are off and running, you'll quickly learn which features you'll need to explore in more detail.

MIDI does not record audio; instead, it records data. Using MIDI, when you play a C on a keyboard, MIDI records which note you played, how long you held the note and how hard you pressed the note. In Sonar, you hear these notes by assigning a VST (Virtual Studio Technology) instrument to the output of the MIDI track. VST is an interface technology that integrates software synthesizers and effects with computer recording systems; VST instruments come in a wide array of options from organs to wind instruments to brass, stringed instruments and of course piano and keyboards. Understanding how to work with MIDI will open a whole new world of adding elements to your creations. For instance, if you hear a melody in your head and can recreate the notes on your MIDI controller, you can then record that MIDI data, assign it a VST and see how it sounds on different instruments. I have put this function to work many times when clients were unsure of an idea working within a song. With MIDI, I can record a part and assign it to an instrument similar to what they are imagining. If they're exploring brass parts, for example, our MIDI track would be assigned to a VST trumpet so we could see if the part was something the client wanted to explore before committing to booking and hiring an actual trumpet player. So, why not just keep the VST trumpet? We could, if the sound is authentic and works in the track. Authentic sounds are available but they can be costly, and it can be tricky to recreate the nuances of a trumpet when playing the part on a keyboard.

Another great benefit of MIDI is it gives you the ability to edit individual notes. When you record audio, you can edit the waveform as a whole but if someone is playing a D chord and messes up the 3rd, you will have to replace the entire chord by recording another take or copying a good one from somewhere else in the song. MIDI, on the other hand, represents each note individually, giving you control over virtually all of the attributes of that note. If the same player messed up that 3rd on a D chord, then you can grab the MIDI note in Sonar and move it into the correct position. You can also make the 3rd of the D chord louder by adjusting its velocity. I realize this may all sound like mumbo-jumbo at this point if you've never worked with MIDI. It is my hope that by the time you finish this chapter, you will have that MIDI "Aha!" moment and you will be as excited as I was when it first hit me. Now, let's look under the hood of MIDI.

First, make sure Sonar recognizes your MIDI interface. We have already discussed the essentials for getting MIDI into our system via a MIDI interface, which can be a standalone unit built into an audio sound card, or even plug directly into the USB port on the computer. To verify that Sonar is ready to play nice with MIDI, go to Options>MIDI Devices. There you will see the recognized MIDI devices. Be sure that the one you want to use is listed with a check next to it (Fig. 26).

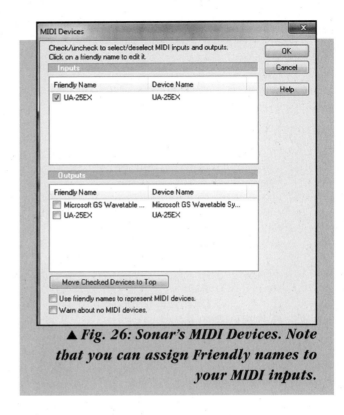

▲ *Fig. 26: Sonar's MIDI Devices. Note that you can assign Friendly names to your MIDI inputs.*

MIDI and Synth Tracks

The next step is to set up a MIDI track. This process works the same way as setting up an audio track. Right-click on the Track Pane and choose New MIDI Track, or navigate to the Insert menu>MIDI Track. You will also need to create a VST track, which houses the VST instrument; Sonar refers to these as Soft Synth Tracks.

A Soft Synth Track houses a synth or a ReWire device. ReWire is a protocol developed by Propellerhead Software and Steinberg for transferring audio data between two computer applications in real time.) Sonar sends the MIDI data to the other app, which processes it through its synth and sends the audio back to Sonar. When you insert a synth into your session you will then be prompted to create the synth track, as well as other options including creating a folder to house the synth track. The synth track can be distinguished visually by a Synth icon next to the track number (Fig. 27).

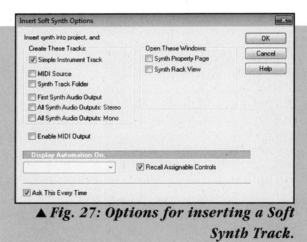

▲ *Fig. 27: Options for inserting a Soft Synth Track.*

To insert a Soft Synth Track, navigate to the Insert Menu, select Soft Synths and choose one of the available Soft Synths. When you insert a Soft Synth Track, you will be presented with a window of options. For our example, check Simple Instrument Track.

Recording MIDI

You've created a MIDI track and routed to the newly created Soft Synth Track. At this point, the hard part is now done—you should hear audio coming through your speakers. Click the R on the MIDI track to arm it, and click the Record button on the large transport. You are now recording MIDI data. The punch-in/-out functions that you learned in the audio section also apply to MIDI.

Editing MIDI

You'll find a few tools to be very handy when working with MIDI. I am going to focus on the best way I have found to begin editing: the Piano Roll screen. To open the piano roll, double-click on the actual MIDI data on the track (Fig. 28).

The Piano Roll screen displays a piano keyboard on the left with the C notes marked. To the right of the keyboard is a grid displaying MIDI data representing the actual notes played, along with velocity and additional channel information. To audition notes, either click on the piano keys or grab a note and move it around.

The Piano Roll includes three primary editing tools from left to right: Select, Draw and Erase (Fig. 29). The Select tool selects notes or controller events. The Draw tool lets you enter, edit and move notes and controller events. Clicking on a blank space in the Piano roll will enter notes; clicking on an existing note will let you drag the note around. The Erase button, when enabled, lets you erase notes or controller events by clicking them.

▲ *Fig. 28: The Piano Roll screen.*

▲ *Fig. 29: MIDI-specific tools.*

Other tools specific to the Piano Roll include the Microscope Mode, which displays a larger zoomed view of the areas you mouse over with your pointer, and Select Controllers, which selects control data along with the notes. When you're working with MIDI, choose Staff view to see a notated representation of your MIDI data. This is helpful if you want to have a printed piece to hand to a musician.

MIDI instructions depend heavily on song tempo, because they draw out notes based on time designation. If you select the Pattern Brush, you'll see a series of note values (whole note, half note, etc.) which will determine note duration when using this tool.

Cleaning up MIDI

Once a MIDI track is recorded it may be necessary
to go back and clean it up. Time for confession: I am
not a pianist. I can get around a bit, but I am not at all
proficient. However, with MIDI, if I can get it close–and
for me, "close" can be a stretch–I can then manually tidy
my work up to match my musical idea.

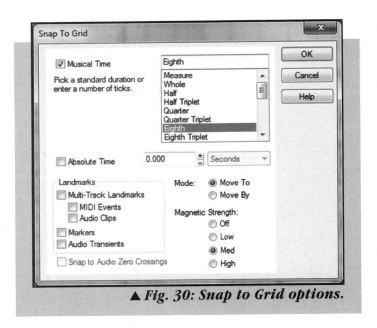

▲ *Fig. 30: Snap to Grid options.*

The Piano Roll overlays a grid to help line up notes.
Using Snap to Grid (enabled by pressing N or clicking
on the Snap to Grid button, which looks like a tic-tac-
toe box), the notes will align to this grid. So, if you
need to tighten up an eighth note, you click on the
small down arrow next to the Snap to Grid button and
choose the eighth note. Now, when you move a note, it
will automatically snap to the nearest eighth-note value.
The Snap to Grid function also works with other editing
functions within the MIDI window (Fig. 30).

Quantizing is a kind of global Snap to Grid applied to all
of the notes selected. To quantize a selection, use your
select tool to draw a box around the notes you would
like to quantize (or press Ctrl-A to select all). From the
Process Menu, choose Quantize. The window shown
here on the right will appear (Fig. 31).

This window lets you define how you want Sonar to
quantize the selected notes. Duration will determine
the time value to match the notes against. If you leave
it set to sixteenth, then each MIDI note start time will
automatically align to the nearest sixteenth note. (For our
purposes, be sure the MIDI Event start times box in the
Change section is selected.)

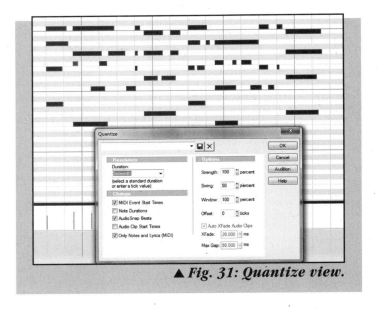

▲ *Fig. 31: Quantize view.*

Other settings determine the "feel" of the quantize.
Quantize is a great feature but depending on the style of the music it can make
things sound too mechanical; experiment with adjusting degree and "swing" of
quantization for a natural, musical feel. Auditioning will let you know how the
quantization will sound.

Remember when we started exploring recording and I talked about
nondestructive editing? Well, this MIDI editing is also nondestructive. Remember
that Ctrl Z equals undo! You will find the Undo feature really useful for testing
quantization values. The best way to learn is to experiment by applying, listening,
undoing, applying, listening and undoing. Repeat until satisfied.

To achieve the exact feel you are looking for, you may have to apply layers of quantization and editing—overall quantization to align the majority of the notes to the right begin time, and individual editing to adjust notes that either quantized to the wrong value (because maybe they were played incorrectly) or landed too early or late in the progression.

There's no one-size-fits-all fix to make MIDI work within your song, nor should there be. The key is to take advantage of all of the available tools, and before you know it you'll be a MIDI editing machine.

Choosing the Right Sound

Now you have a MIDI track that feels pretty good. This is where exploring the available sounds can come in hand and where you can start combining different sounds together to make the perfect blend.

To audition sounds, launch the Synth Rack, which can be found under the Views Menu>Synth Rack or by pressing Alt-8 (Fig. 32). This rack is the main hub for all things synth. Here you can add synths, edit the current synth and automate certain features.

To edit the current synth, double-click on the picture associated with that synth. Your next menu will vary depending on the synth itself and how it was designed. Some synths have no controls, only presets; some have no presets, only controls. When starting off, I will usually try to find a preset that is in the ballpark of the sound I'm looking for and tweak the sound to my heart's desire. This can be a bit of an inexact science until you get familiar with the parameters. Once you find something that you like, most synths will allow you to save that preset so you can use it again or at least load it for a future starting point.

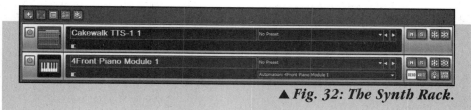

▲ *Fig. 32: The Synth Rack.*

If you decide to try another synth altogether, click on the "+" button and choose from the list of available synths. Remember, you will need to go back to the MIDI track itself and route the output into the new synth's input. Then you can start searching and editing the presets associated with that synth.

One arrangement tip: If you right-click on your MIDI track and choose Clone Track, a new track will be created with the same MIDI notes. It is sometimes cool to build up an arrangement this way and then add or subtract notes from the cloned track while routing it to a different synth sound. This technique is a good way to experiment with blending sounds without having to play each track multiple times and get it right every time. It won't work for every creation, but you never know what you may land upon.

Synth Freeze

Using too many synths can tax system resources; if you want to avoid running into performance glitches, right-click on the MIDI or Synth Track Pane and choose Freeze. Just like with your audio track, this function will process the MIDI track through the synth and create an audio track. It will then turn off that particular synth and free up some resources. If you decide to edit the MIDI or sound again, right-clicking on Unfreeze will let you get back into the synth and MIDI data for more editing.

MIDI Review

Let's recap what you have learned—I may even drop
in a couple of other nuggets, just to make sure you are still paying attention.

- MIDI, unlike audio, records data.

- In Sonar, MIDI tracks record MIDI data, which is then routed to a Synth Track.

- A virtual instrument provides sounds for MIDI notes. These sounds offer a great way to experiment with things that are not always available using audio tracks.

- The Piano Roll view is the primary way to edit MIDI data in Sonar.

- The Snap to Grid feature will snap notes to the nearest predetermined value.

- Pressing the "I" key will turn the visual grid on and off; this grid is also editable by clicking the small arrow next to the grid button with a picture of a folder inside it.

- A combination of Quantize and manual editing will most likely yield the best results for a natural-feeling track.

- Freezing MIDI tracks will temporarily free up system resources for other uses.

- The Synth Track is the home for all of your MIDI sound modules.

CHAPTER 9   MIXING IN SONAR

Now you're ready for the final step to bring everything together: mixing. This is when you will set levels, create envelopes, apply equalization (EQ) and effects and work to combine all of these different elements, both MIDI and audio, for a unified sound. It takes some practice to get things sounding the way you want, but with a little patience and ear training, you are well on your way to completing your song.

Where to Start

Before officially beginning the mixing process, you should have completed the majority of edits, including comping instruments and vocals, tuning, etc. Granted, you may end up doing some editing once you are into the mix, but you will approach that work from a different perspective.

When you begin to mix, organization is key. Before I start, I prefer to have all of my tracks laid out, cleaned up, routed and labeled. I even attach cool graphics to the track so I can easily identify the audio on each track.

Track Folders are fantastic for organizing your tracks. To use them, right-click in the Track Pane and choose Insert Track Folder. Then, drag anything you want into that folder. Expand or contract the folder for easier viewing in track view. The Track Folder also has dedicated Mute, Solo and Archive buttons, which apply to every track within that folder. Track Folders are very common for drums, background vocals, and any other multiple tracks that are similar in nature. Since Track Folders are meant for organization, they do not have any processing options (Fig. 33).

▲ *Fig. 33: Track Folder showing three vocal tracks nested within the folder*

Another form of organization that may seem a little over the top for some, but I have found worth taking the time to set up, is using track icons, which are small pictures that represent the tracks' assigned instruments. Track Icons appear at the bottom of the track in Console View and on the Track inspector in the Track View.

To add icons, right-click on the default picture located below the fader and choose Load Track Icon. The default Track Icon folder will open. Browse to the icon that best describes your instrument and double-click it to choose it. You can also create custom icons and place them in the Track Icon folder (Fig. 34).

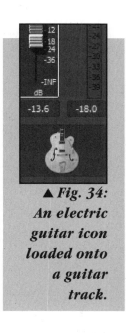

▲ *Fig. 34: An electric guitar icon loaded onto a guitar track.*

Console View

Let's take a look at Sonar's Console View (Alt-3). This window will be your primary workspace during the mixing process, with some Track View (Alt-0) sprinkled in along the way (Fig. 35).

In the Console View, look at the far-left side of the screen. There, you will see the Show/Hide strip control, which is where you determine which console elements are viewable from within this window. If you find you don't need to see some of these items, deselecting them will free up the window space. If you have to scroll up or down to view everything in the Console View, then you might want to hide some of these items from your current view (Fig. 36).

▲ *Fig. 35: Sonar's primary workspace for mixing: the Console View.*

▲ *Fig. 36: The Console View's Show/ Hide strip control buttons.*

The Show/Hide strip controls buttons labeled Tracks, Buses and Mains. The Tracks are what you have recorded, while Buses route tracks and Mains are the main outputs.

The Audio Track Strip

Anytime I teach someone to operate a mixing console, whether it is a software or hardware device, I always break it down into sections. I'll start with the Audio Track strip (Fig. 37).

Once you learn the functions of one strip, you'll know the functions of all of the strips. Don't be intimidated by what may look like a ton of buttons and knobs; you've made it this far! I'll explain the strip, working from the top down (for my Track View, I hid the input section):

▲ *Fig. 37: Audio Track strip.*

- The EQ Section: Each track has its own equalizer (Fig. 38).

▲ *Fig. 38*

- FX Bin: Each track can have its own dedicated FX, or you can route tracks to buses where you can insert FX for multiple tracks to share (Fig. 39).

▲ *Fig. 39*

- Auxiliary (Aux) Sends: Use these to send a copy of the track to a bus in order to apply effects to the bus independently from the track (Fig. 40).

▲ *Fig. 40*

- Fader section: Here, you control automation recording, left-right pan position, volume and track output routing (Fig. 41).

▲ *Fig. 41*

- Track Icon: This visual reference helps you quickly identify and organize tracks (Fig. 42).

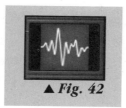

▲ *Fig. 42*

Get On the Bus!

Buses route numerous tracks together. Buses have two primary functions: track organization and routing. Bus tracks are laid out very much like individual tracks; the main difference is bus tracks do not have any audio directly associated with them. The aux section mentioned above is a bus, the main outputs are a bus, the bus tracks are a bus. If I have multiple tracks of the same type of instrument, like drums, I will make a bus called Kit and route all of my drums to that bus. I'll use the individual tracks to get the correct blend, but with everything routed to one bus, multiple tracks are much easier to manage.

Buses are also used for creative workflow. You can take, say, a vocal, and keep the original vocal track with EQ and effects, route a copy to another bus or two which have their own dedicated EQ and effects, and combine the two together to make one smoking hot vocal track. And, with buses, you can keep combining until your machine processing power runs out.

At this point, I will usually create my buses with a rough idea based on the session. For the session on the DVD, I'd like one for vocal effects, one for the loop and one for piano. Again, buses can be added as needed, but this will give us a good start.

In the right side of the Console view, right-click Add New Stereo Bus. Once you have created all three buses, name them Vocal FX, Kit FX and Piano FX. Be sure the outputs of those buses are routed to the main output.

Now, go to the primary vocal track. Right-click in the Aux Send section and choose Vocal FX. Sonar creates an aux send that is routed to the Vocal FX bus. Make sure it is set to On and that the Post button is lit. Now, when you press Play, you should see signal on the Vocal track and on the Vocal FX bus.

Note that audio effects will not apply to MIDI tracks, nor will bus routing work on MIDI tracks. MIDI tracks must be routed to a synth track, which can then turn the MIDI notes into audio. You can record that audio track and add processing, or route the synth output to a bus and apply processing.

Envelopes and Automation

Managing dynamic levels is an important part of mixing. To shape volume, you'll need to "ride the faders"; this phrase refers to the days when there was a physical fader associated with every track. The engineer would ride the fader with his finger during playback, and record those fader moves so that the performance fit well in the track. Now, we can ride the fader with a mouse. Setting the fader's automation to Write mode and moving the fader or manually playing dot-to-dot with track envelopes will do the trick. (To create an envelope on a track or bus, switch to the Track View and right-click on the track.)

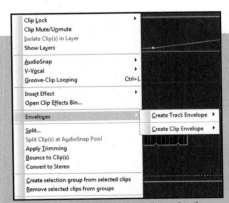

▲ Fig. 43: Right-click on any track or bus to create an envelope.

You can create an envelope for an entire track or just a clip of audio. The types of envelopes available depend on what you have plugged into and activated on that track. Every track will have an envelope for Volume and Pan. Volume is self-explanatory. The Pan function determines where that track fits in the stereo field, ranging from left to right. Pan can be set above the fader if the track's pan settings do not change for the entire song. If they do, you will need to automate those settings.

Create an envelope for the volume; you will now see a line over your track. To make changes, double-click on the line to put a dot on the line (when using the Select tool). Each of those dots can be grabbed with the mouse and dragged up and down, representing changes in volume level. Add as many dots as you need; Sonar has an Envelope draw tool to assist with more complex manual entries (Fig. 44).

▲ *Fig. 44:*
Envelope Tools
in Sonar.

Pressing the W in the track pane will enable the track to write the automation; you do not have to punch Record on the transport. As soon as you start playback and "touch" the fader with the mouse, the automation will start writing, and the RD button will read the automation. If this button is turned off, any moves—whether drawn in or written with fader moves—will be ignored.

Automation and envelopes can be applied to both tracks and buses. The bus option is handy when routing multiple instruments—say, all of your rhythm electric guitars—to one bus. Using a combination of writing and drawing envelopes, I now have automated all of my guitars with the same fader moves on one track—very handy, indeed.

At any point, you can right-click on an automation point to delete it, or draw a box around multiple automation points with the Envelope tool and delete the points within the box.

Effects Overview

I want to hit a brief overview on the most common effects used for mixing. To do this, I am going to share excerpts from *Teach Yourself Mixing* by David A. Terry. This book is a comprehensive look at mixing, and I highly recommend it for you to take your mixes to the next level (see page 59).

Reverb

Reverb can be used for creating a natural-sounding space in your individual tracks, adding wacky special effects or for making things sound farther back in the mix. There are many different types of reverb signal processors, including plates, rooms, spring reverbs and convolution reverbs. Many commercial mixing studios have dedicated reverb units. In the not-too-distant past, using these types of units was the only way to get good-quality-sounding reverbs while mixing. Today, however, there are scads of high-quality reverb plug-ins available for use in digital audio workstations. Whether you are using computers or an old-school dedicated plate reverb, the concepts and controls apply (Fig. 45).

▲ *Fig. 45: Sonar ships*
with the Lexicon
Pantheon Reverb multi-
preset reverb plug-in, a
good starting point for
adding reverb, with a
simple interface.

Normally, you will use a few reverbs in a mix and route multiple instruments through those few reverbs. The rationale behind using a few reverbs for the entire mix, rather than a different reverb for every track, is to give the separate tracks some cohesion and to save on resources. You also want many instruments to sound like they are in the same space, to give the mix a glued-together effect. Set this up by using effects sends and returns. Most analog and digital mixing consoles have a few dedicated effects sends/returns and/or auxiliary sends/returns. If you are working on a computer-based workstation these can be set up easily, just by creating the necessary tracks.

Delay

Delay…..-delay…..-lay…...-lay…...-lay…processors record an audio signal, then play it back after a user-defined period of time. The delayed signal may be played back multiple times and/or played back into the original signal. This creates a repeating, decaying echo effect. Like reverbs, delays can be used for creating a sense of space in the mix or for achieving other special effects.

If your reverb choices aren't quite working for you, try using a delay! Or use delays and reverbs together. I almost always use a combination of delays and reverbs to achieve a sense of space and dimension in the mix. Short delay times with a low feedback setting provide a slap-back sort of effect. Longer delay times with a higher feedback setting are what you might typically associate with a big haired rock guitar solo. Multiple mono delays, panned hard-left and hard-right with different delay times, can really widen the stereo image of any source. Vocals and delays go together like chocolate and peanut butter. You can set up a delay using aux sends and returns in the same manner as you did the reverb. Or, you can use them as an insert on a specific audio track. I'd say that 80% of the time I use the aux send approach for delays (Fig. 46).

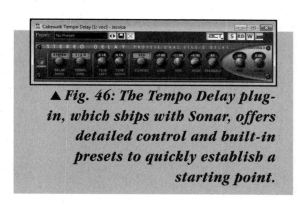

▲ *Fig. 46: The Tempo Delay plug-in, which ships with Sonar, offers detailed control and built-in presets to quickly establish a starting point.*

Modulation Effects

Modulation effects include flangers, choruses, phasers, tremolos, vibratos and rotary-type processors. These processors are all similar in that they all create some type of sweeping, swooshing or pulsing effect that can create a wider stereo image. They can simulate outer space sounds, Leslie speaker cabinets, totally bizarre robot-type effects, or even do simple doubling. The most widely used modulation effects are choruses, phasers and flangers. These types of modulation effects add a pitch-shifted, delayed version of the signal to the original signal. These type of effects were originally intended to give the sense of multiple instruments playing the same part at the same time. While using chorus, phase and flange effects will give the sense of a bigger and wider sound, they will also cause a less-defined washy-ness within the context of the mix. Phase and pitch shifting can also cause some phase cancellation when summed to mono, so you should be aware of the pitfalls as well as the pleasures of using these tools.

Dynamics Overview

Where effects deal with time and space, dynamics processors deal with loudness of the total sound or of selected frequency components by either adjusting overall volume boosting or cutting frequencies. Here's more from *Teach Yourself Mixing*:

Equalization

There used to be a TV show in the '80s about a gun-toting vigilante called The Equalizer, *but that is not what I'm referring to here. An EQ, or equalizer, is a filter or set of filters that allows you to alter the frequency content of an audio signal in some way. Like oil filters remove unwanted dirt particles from your car's engine, these EQ filters are used for removing unwanted noise, compensating for unbalanced frequencies, improving fidelity or emphasizing a frequency area. They can even be used as a creative tool to make your amazing acoustic guitar sound like it was recorded underwater through a telephone.*

EQs not only remove unwanted frequencies from specific instruments or stereo mixes, but they can also affect the physical perception or distance of elements in the mix. Bright instruments or instruments with more high-frequency information are perceived as being closer and more up-front in the mix, while darker ones are sensed as being more distant. By using a high-shelving EQ and cutting high frequencies, you can effectively push things farther back in your mix. Likewise, boosting the upper mids and/or high frequencies will bring things more up front and in your face.

Compressors

Compressors are devices that reduce the dynamic range of audio signals. Louder sounds over a defined threshold are reduced in level (compressed), while quieter sounds below the threshold are left unaffected. Simply put, a compressor is an automatic volume control. In addition to controlling volume, compressors can be used for more creative tasks, such as tone control boxes, sibilance removers, distortion generators and automatic mother-in-law loudness fixers.

Compressors are probably the most powerful and effective devices that are used to make a great mix. They are also the easiest things to overuse and abuse. Compression will bring up the noise floor so that noise that was unnoticeable during recording suddenly becomes very apparent after compression is applied. They can also make elements sit in just the right place in the mix when used correctly. There is no right amount of compression, nor is there a "one size fits all" approach to compressor settings. After reading this section, spend time experimenting and trying different approaches. Do lots of listening to learn how compressors can enhance or degrade your mix. Also keep in mind that compressors and EQs need to work in tandem. Compression changes the sound of the source, so the tonal shape of the source is going to most likely be different after compression is applied. Also, changing an EQ setting that is inserted before the compressor is going to change how the compressor behaves. For example, if you apply a 10 dB boost at 2,000 Hz on a vocal (why would anyone do that?), the compressor that is inserted after the EQ is going to be triggered off the massive boost at that frequency. Likewise, cutting frequencies before hitting the compressor will result in the compressor entering compression later than it normally would.

De-Essing

De-essing is the process of removing unwanted sibilance or "essess" from a vocal performance. Ideally, the vocals will be recorded in a way that de-essing isn't necessary. But some vocalists just sing with a very pronounced "sss" in their delivery, which has to be dealt with during the mixing process.

Adding Effects and Dynamic Processing

Each version of Sonar comes equipped with both effects and dynamic processing. Producer (which was used for this book and DVD set) comes with a strong palette of options, including a long list of virtual synthesizers, amp and tape simulators. For dynamics processing, the VC-64 Vintage Channel is a great, quick go-to effect, and the new VX-64 Vocal Strip is a fantastic all-in-one processor designed specifically for vocals. Master tools include a multiband linear phase compressor and a high-end linear phase graphic EQ. Needless to say, Sonar will provide you with a versatile list of effects, synths and processors right out of the box. However, there will come a time where you want the option to expand your palette; there are many third-party VST plug-ins on the market, as well as free VST plug-ins on the internet.

There are a number of ways to add processing in Sonar: on the track, bus, master fader or via a combination of these steps. Remember, you're only limited by the amount of available processing on your computer. Wherever you add processing, the steps are the same: right-click on the FX bin of the track, either in Track or Console view. In the next menu, scroll down to Audio FX and choose from the available plug-ins. The order you insert your plug-ins is the order in which the audio will be processed. If you insert a compressor, reverb and EQ, then the audio will first go through the compressor, then the reverb, then the EQ. If you want your effects to take place in a different order, click and drag plug-ins to change them around. To compare a track with and without a plug-in, toggle the green box next to the plug-in name. (Green means active.) Right-click on a plug-in if you want to delete it from the track altogether (Fig. 47).

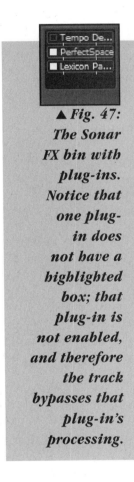

▲ *Fig. 47: The Sonar FX bin with plug-ins. Notice that one plug-in does not have a highlighted box; that plug-in is not enabled, and therefore the track bypasses that plug-in's processing.*

EQ in Sonar

Each track is equipped with its own onboard EQ, which you can use instead of, or in conjunction with, a plug-in EQ. To use the track's onboard EQ, right-click on the EQ graph in the EQ bin and choose Enable EQ. Notice that you can also assign the EQ pre (before) or post (after) the FX bin (Fig. 48).

When the EQ is enabled, the Enable button will turn green. Click on the down arrow next to Band 1, and notice that there are four bands available. (A band is an adjustable frequency range.) Below band 1, choose the EQ type. Then, you can adjust the knobs on the EQ to change the graph, but I like to see what I am doing while I'm listening. Working

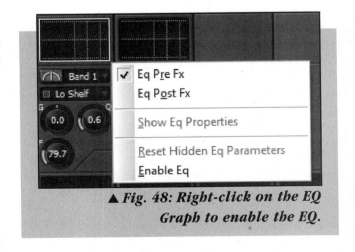

▲ *Fig. 48: Right-click on the EQ Graph to enable the EQ.*

visually helps you associate the image you are seeing with the sound you are hearing, and soon you will be able to identify frequencies more easily because you are not just blindly adjusting knobs.

To work in the visual mode, double-click on the EQ graph. Sonar's own Sonitus equalizer will appear, displaying a graph with adjustments below it. To enable a band, double-click on the numbered dot in the graph, then adjust. Continue with all six bands, or with any combination of bands. Next to the faders are additional adjustments such as the Q (an expression of bandwidth), filter type, selected frequency and amount of addition or subtraction (Fig. 49).

If you aren't sure where to start, a preset menu can serve as a good starting point. Once you find something you like, you can save it as a preset for use in another track, or even another session somewhere down the line.

▲ *Fig. 49: The Sonitus equalizer is part of an effects suite that ships with Sonar.*

CHAPTER 10   MASTERING IN SONAR

The final step in production is mastering. Mastering is a specialized art form. Where mixing the music deals with multiple tracks, and making them into a stereo mix, mastering involves taking a stereo mix through processing and editing, and optimizes how the end result ultimately sounds. A good mastering engineer is invaluable especially when working with an entire album. They will work with each of the songs to make the whole project flow seamlessly. This section is not a comprehensive guide to mastering, as that in itself could easily take a whole book, but is a good starting point to understanding what happens with a stereo mix of your recordings during the mastering process.

The price for a good mastering engineer can easily start at $2500 per album of ten or so songs. This kind of expense is not always an option with home-recording musicians, so some self-mastering is sometimes required, and Sonar offers some great tools you can use to do the job. These can be used as plug-ins on the stereo mix output when you export your mix, or better yet, you can import a final stereo track into a new Sonar Session for the mastering process. The latter is ideal because the mastering tools require a good deal of CPU processing power. Start the process by exporting your final stereo mix and then importing that mix back into a stereo track on a new session. Set the fader level to 0 so the overall output is not changed from your final mix level.

The next step is working with plug-ins on the final mix. Sonar Producer ships with the most tools for mastering, with Sonar Studio only having a couple of plug-ins specifically designed for mastering. What separates a mastering plug-in from a normal plug-in? Tools designed for mastering are generally for more precise adjustments. However, there is nothing wrong with trying some of your favorite plug-ins, either Sonar provided or third party, for mastering just as there is no reason to not try a mastering plug-in on a standard audio track. However, mastering plug-ins generally do require more DSP (digital signal processing) which means they will use up more of your CPU and memory.

Here is an overview of some of the plug-ins included in Sonar.

LP Multiband 64

The LP Multiband 64 (see Fig. 50) is a multi-band compressor. Where a standard compressor generally deals with the entirety of an audio track, a multi-band compressor can address different frequency ranges with different compression algorithms. In the case of the LP 64, there are 5 bands of compression available all with precision adjustments for each of the settings. If a track's low end is not quite thumping enough, a good mastering engineer can put one of these to use to hit the compressor a little harder in the 60-80Hz frequency range and help it jump out a bit more in the track. Conversely, if a frequency range is too out front, this tool can be used to address that problem as well. Each of the compressors has a red S button which allows the user to Solo up just that band of compression. This is a great help if you are trying to locate a specific frequency range. The E key is also a key player in that button will enable/disable that frequency band. You always want to master with the whole picture in mind so after making a detailed tweak on a section you have honed into, be sure to back out to see how it plays out in the big picture of the song.

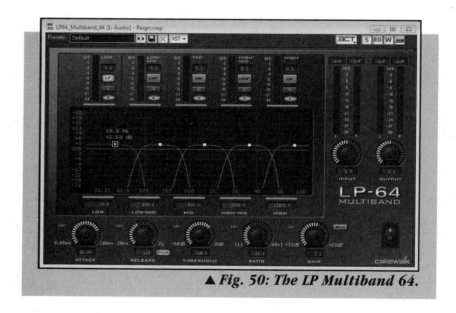

▲ *Fig. 50: The LP Multiband 64.*

LP 64 EQ

The LP 64 EQ (Fig. 51) is a linear phase EQ offered in the Producer Edition of Sonar. This is not a fixed graphic EQ even though at first glance it may appear to be one. A fixed graphic EQ has set frequencies for adjusting. To add a frequency, just double-click on the EQ bar. This will insert a small white block on the bar. That block can be dragged back and forth, up and down, to land on the exact frequency that you want to adjust. The bottom of the EQ window also shows a Q box. The Q indicates how wide the frequency range is that you are adjusting. The higher the Q number, the smaller the range of affected frequencies. Clicking on the Default listing in the upper left-hand window will show a list of presets to load which are designed to address specific areas. If your vocal part is biting a bit too much, you can choose the De-Harsh Vocal preset and this will serve as a good starting point for removing the harshness from the sound, even in a mix.

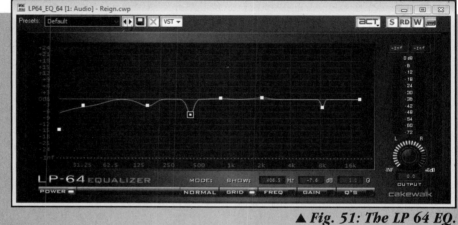

▲ *Fig. 51: The LP 64 EQ.*

Boost 11

Have you ever noticed how "loud" songs sound on the radio as opposed to your final mixes? That effect can be majorly attributed to a good mastering engineer who was able to squeeze all of the level they could out of the final mix. Sonar (Producer and Studio) offer a tool designed specifically for this purpose, called Boost 11 (Fig. 52). This is a very simple peak limiter to use, but be careful of overdriving and causing distortion on the output. Basically, there is an input section and an output section. The interface offers a view of the waveforms as well as controls for the levels.

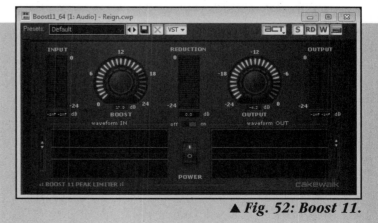

▲ *Fig. 52: Boost 11.*

TL-64 Tube Leveler

Sometimes a final mastering session is as much about adding color to a mix as it is ascertaining what frequencies need to be adjusted and/or compressed. The TL-64 Tube Leveler (Fig. 53, found in Sonar Producer) is a line driver/leveling processor which encompasses an analog-tube modeling feature designed to add what some refer to as "warmth" to a track. The warmth is associated with the days of actual tubes which became popular, and are still very popular in many audio devices, because the tube circuitry would round off the edges naturally. The TL-64 Tube Leveler is also equipped with presets to help the user quickly try to land a good starting point. It is broken down into four sections; input, dynamics, saturation and output gain. Not to be too non-technical with this one, but this is one of those plug-ins where it just takes some time and experiments in tweaking the settings to make more sense of how each section affects the overall mix.

▲ *Fig. 53: The TL-64 Tube Leveler.*

Sonar offers other tools to help with this process and as I stated earlier, any tool can be used for mastering if it ultimately provides the desired end result. If it sounds right, it is right. Sometimes it requires some experimentation and if time allows, I recommend a lot of experimentation. Remember, every step that doesn't work out is just one step closer to the one that does.

The final element that the mastering engineers will sometimes do is editing such as fade in and outs, album track order (what songs flow well into other songs) and even replacing parts within your songs from different mix versions. What that means is that the vocal in the chorus may seem a bit buried as compared to the vocal in the verse, so the mastering engineer could ask to have you print a version with the vocal up 1dB throughout the whole song. This is easily done by raising the volume envelope by 1 dB on the vocal track or bus master, depending how you chose to route the vocals during the mix. Then the mastering engineer will cut out the chorus with the buried vocal and put in the chorus from the +1dB vocal mix.

Monitoring

▲ *Fig. 54: KRK's line of Rokit Powered RPG2 Speakers — a good source of monitoring is imperative for mixing and mastering.*

Probably the most important component, other than your ears, is listening, listening, listening, and not just on the same speakers. I will usually burn a CD and check final mixes and mastered mixes in my car, in my office, on my computer, on my home system, on my favorite headphones, systems with subwoofers and wherever else I find myself listening to music. Pass it onto friends whose ears and taste in music you trust. Many times I will print multiple masters of the same track, each with different tweaks applied, so I can compare them back to back on similar systems. Bottom line, listen to your mix in a lot of places, because you may find that you've mixed and mastered your recording so that it sounds great on your home studio speakers, and sounds terrible on other systems. Make notes when you listen on other systems, and go back and make adjustments to your mixes while referring to your notes. Did the bass drop out in your car stereo system? Is the bass overpowering in your car? What about in a friend's car? How does it sound through your home stereo or media playback system in your living room? Listen, take notes, re-mix and re-master, until it sounds great on all of them.

Be sure to rest your ears often and don't jump right into a mastering session after you finish the mix, at least not on the same song. Fatigue will always hamper your ability to critically listen to any music. I recommend living with your final mixes for at least a day or two, compare them with other music you like, then go back and make changes based on what you observed on other systems. If you can hire an outside mastering engineer it is always good to get another set of ears to do this detailed work. Or, if you find yourself with the gift of critical listening and enjoying microscopic tweaking, you may be able to turn this whole mastering thing into another way to create some income.

The Final Step: Printing the Mix

So, you've followed all of the steps, experimented and tweaked yourself silly, and you want to "print" a mix to listen on different systems and play for your friends to get their opinions. To do this, you have to choose which elements you want Sonar to mix down. Mixing down, or Exporting, is taking what you hear when you are playing back your mix and creating a stereo file to burn to CD or other medium.

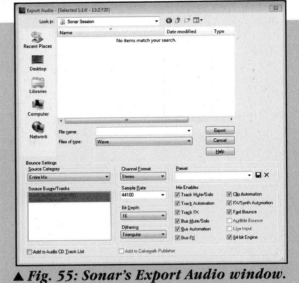

Press Ctrl-A to select everything in your session. In the File menu, choose Export>Audio. The next window will let you name and save the file (Fig. 55). There are a plethora of export options. For this example, we will choose CD quality, which is a sample rate of 44,100 Hz (or 44.1 kHz) and bit depth of 16. We will keep the default settings of a stereo track and all of the available check boxes selected. Name the file, choose the file type and press Export. Sonar will display a progress bar at the bottom of your session. When that progress bar is complete, so is your mix! Listen to your new mix file and confirm that it sounds the same as your Sonar session did. If something is awry, confirm that you selected all of your tracks and no tracks are inadvertently muted.

▲ *Fig. 55: Sonar's Export Audio window.*

Let's say you only want to mix down one track or a series of tracks—say, drums and bass, to get an idea of how your rhythm section sounds as a whole. Or maybe you want to email the file to a guitarist to add in some tracks. In the source category, select Tracks and choose the tracks you want to export.

These steps are the basics for mixing, and they also act as tools for your most important step—listening. Listen to different recordings that you enjoy as references; listen to your mix on different speakers in different environments. (I, for one, love my car stereo! Next to my studio speakers, I listen here the most, since I spend the most time listening to all types of music in my car.) Other options include home stereo systems, MP3 players, ear buds/headphones, computers, whatever you have that you are familiar with; use them all to reference your mix.

FINAL TAKE

Hopefully you now have your head around Sonar's basic functions and can dig into it on your own. Making the most of Sonar will ultimately depend on the type of music and instrumentation your project requires. It is my hope this book serves as an informative on-ramp to all of Sonar's capabilities.

Sonar is not a difficult program to learn, and the Help files (shortcut: F1) that come with the system are exceptionally good. But aside from fooling around with some projects to learn how to use the application's features, you'll get the best results if you bring a great song, with a thought-out, rehearsed, enthusiastic and emotional performance.

Like anything that you set out to become good at, practice is the key to becoming more fluent and working more smoothly and quickly in Sonar. The more you practice, the more the technical issues will blend into the background and the creativity will move into focus. Enjoy your journey, and may you make recordings to your heart's desire!

ABOUT THE AUTHOR

Dan Wothke has accrued more than 15 years of studio and live sound experience. He originally cut his audio teeth as the chief engineer for an independent record label, followed by the role of technician at Masterfonics Tracking Room; he has engineered live broadcasts and tours along the way. Wothke is Media Director at Belmont Church in Nashville, works as a freelance engineer, and regularly reviews audio equipment and writes a House of Worship feature for *Pro Audio Review*.

He lives outside Nashville with his wife and two children.

Learn more about Dan Wothke at:

http://www.wothke.com

NOTES

INDEX